D0342634

RECORDing and PROMOTing YOUR music

Matt Anniss

Chicago, Illinois

Edited by Clare Lewis, Mandy Robbins,
Penny West, and James Benefield
Designed by Steve Mead
Original illustrations © Capstone Global Library
Ltd 2015
Picture research by Ruth Blair
Production by Victoria Fitzgerald
Originated by Capstone Global Library Ltd
Printed and bound in China by CTPS

18 17 16 15 14
10 9 8 7 6 5 4 3 2 1

Library of Congress Cataloging-in-Publication Data
Anniss, Matt, author.
  Recording and promoting your music /
Matthew Anniss.
       pages cm.—(I'm in the band)
  Includes bibliographical references and index.
  ISBN 978-1-4109-6726-8 (hb)—ISBN 978-1-
4109-6731-2 (pb) 1. Rock music—Vocational
guidance—Juvenile literature. 2. Sound
recordings—Production and direction—Juvenile
literature. 3. Music trade—Vocational guidance—
Juvenile literature. I. Title.
  ML3795.A857 2015
  780.23—dc23   2013042107

Acknowledgments
We would like to thank the following for
permission to reproduce photographs: Alamy p.
9 (© Marc Tielemans); Corbis pp. 23 (© Frederic
Pitchal/Sygma), 29 (© Hill Street Studios/Blend
Images/); Getty Images pp. 4, 5, 28 (Henrik
Sorensen), 6 (Matt Kent/WireImage), 7 (Jesse
Wild/Computer Music magazine), 10 (Gregg
DeGuire/FilmMagic), 12 (Joseph Branston/Total
Guitar magazine), 13 (Joby Sessions/Classic
Rock Magazine/TeamRock), 16 (Tony Hopewell),
18 (Gabriel Olsen), 19 (Tim Mosenfelder), 20
(Kevin Mazur), 21 (Mark Metcalfe), 26 (George
Rose), 31 (Laurence Griffiths), 32 (Jemal
Countess), 33 (Jerod Harris), 34 (Mike Windle/
ACMA2013/Getty Images for ACM), 35 (OSCAR
SIAGIAN/AFP), 36 (Westend61), 37 (Chelsea
Lauren/WireImage), 38 (Chris McKay/WireImage),
39 (Tim Mosenfelder), 40 (Kevin Winter/
WireImage), 41 (Dave J Hogan); Shutterstock
pp. 8 bottom (Africa Studio), 8 middle left (8
middle left), 8 middle right (Olena Zaskochenko),
8 top (ollyy), 11 (Monkey Business Images), 17
(leungchopan), 22 (Sergey Goruppa), 27 (Adam
J. Sablich).

Artistic Effects: Shutterstock.

Cover photograph reproduced with permission of
Getty Images (Tetra Images).

CONTENTS

Do It Yourself 4

Recording Your Music 6

Releasing Your Music 16

Promoting Your Music 26

Building a Fan Base 34

Quiz 42

Glossary 44

Find Out More 46

Index 48

Do It Yourself

If you make music, you want your songs to be heard by as many people as possible. You want to travel the world, playing your music to thousands of excited fans. You want people to tell their friends to take a look at your latest video on YouTube. You want all these things, but above all you want to be successful. This is what every musician wants, but in reality, very few get to achieve the dream. For every band packing huge stadiums around the world, there are thousands of others who are barely known in their hometown, let alone across the globe.

Changing times

The good news is that things are changing. In the old days, huge international companies called record labels had the power to make musicians into stars. They could take someone from obscurity to worldwide fame in a matter of months, usually by spending huge amounts of money. This can still happen, but there are other ways of making it big...

You don't need record labels, or even large amounts of money, to become a successful musician these days. Thanks to cheaper musical equipment, easier methods of recording, and the wonder of the Internet, you can forge a successful musical career from the comfort of your bedroom. This book will explain how to do just that—and have lots of fun in the process.

IF YOU FOLLOW THE ADVICE IN THIS BOOK, IT COULD BE YOU UP ONSTAGE!

According to music industry research, the average amount of money spent by a big record label on launching the career of a big musician is between $770,000 and $1.5 million!

Did you know?

kECORDING YOUk MUSIC

If you want to promote your music and find new fans, you will need something that people can listen to whenever they want to. You need something that prospective fans can download to their phones, computers, and MP3 players—something that can be accessed 24 hours a day on the Internet. To be able to let people listen, you will need to record your music.

Recording basics

The basic idea of recording is to create a track that best shows off your music. You want your songs to sound fantastic, with every instrument and voice playing its part. If you get it right, there is more of a chance that listeners will be impressed and want to hear more.

BANDS SUCH AS BIFFY CLYRO OFTEN RECORD SIMPLE ACOUSTIC VERSIONS OF THEIR SONGS USING BASIC INSTRUMENTS.

There are many different ways to record your music. You could play together, as a band, and record the results on a portable MP3 player. You could record all of the instruments and vocals (the singing) separately, and then put them together later, using a process called mixing. You can even use a computer to put your song together, piece by piece.

DANCE PRODUCER DOM KANE RECORDS MOST OF HIS MUSIC USING A MAC COMPUTER AND A COUPLE OF KEYBOARDS.

BANDSPEAK

Mixing is the last stage of recording. It is the process of deciding how each element in your recording will sound, before making tiny adjustments. Once a track has been "mixed down," it is finished.

Take a little time

Whichever method you choose, be prepared for the recording process to take longer than you expect. It can take experienced bands days, weeks, or even months to produce great recordings of their songs. If you take your time, there will be more chance of you getting it right.

Home recording

Famous bands and singers usually record their songs in large recording studios, which are special places designed solely for the purpose of recording music. However, using recording studios is expensive, so most bands start out by making recordings at home.

Portable studio

There are many ways to record your music at home. One of the most popular is to use a portable multitrack recorder. This is a small device designed to record performances quickly and easily. Multitrack recorders are relatively inexpensive.

Portable recorders are also popular with famous bands and singers, who use them to record early versions of new songs. In music circles, these home recordings are often referred to as "demos" (which is short for demonstrations). You can find home demos from the likes of The Strokes and Muse on YouTube.

BAND TECH

Multitrack recording gets its name because it allows you to record several different sound sources at the same time. Each instrument or microphone is given its own separate "track" to record onto. The number of "tracks" available to record onto differs from recorder to recorder, but usually ranges from four ("four-track") to sixteen ("sixteen-track").

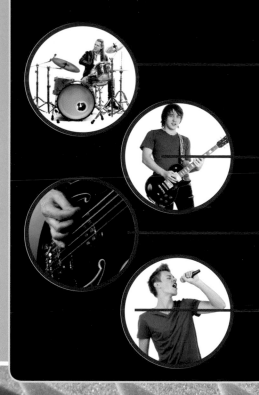

TRACKS

Each of these is capable of recording a separate instrument or microphone.

TRACK RECORD

Use these buttons to decide which tracks you want to record on at any given time.

MENU SCREEN

During recording, this shows how long you've been recording for and how loud the recording is.

TRACK VOLUME

This can be used to change the loudness of the sound from each instrument during recording.

MASTER RECORD

When you press this, you start recording. Get playing!

PLAYBACK

Press this to listen back to your recordings.

Music and technology

Today, many people prefer to record music using computers, tablets (such as the iPad), and even cell phones. Rap and dance music bands have used computers to record their songs for years, but today many pop and rock bands also use them.

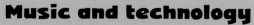

ALTHOUGH DAFT PUNK'S RECENT ALBUMS HAVE BEEN RECORDED IN EXPENSIVE STUDIOS, THEY FIRST MADE THEIR NAME WITH TRACKS CREATED ON A COMPUTER.

Electronic equipment

Some musicians create their tracks entirely on computers and do not even play traditional instruments such as guitars and drums. Instead, they use a keyboard connected to their computer to play in music, which can then be altered and changed to sound like almost anything, from violins, harps, and saxophones to futuristic synthesizers and grand pianos. Songs are recorded and arranged using a computer music recording application, such as GarageBand, Logic Pro, Cubase, or Reason.

Keeping it real

If you want to record real instruments in a song you are creating on a computer, you can do this using something called a sound card. This turns sound into information that computers can understand, and vice versa. Some computers come with a built-in sound card. If your computer doesn't, you can buy a separate, "external" sound card to plug in.

Anything goes

There are many benefits to using computers to record your songs. Although it may take a little longer, computer recording gives you greater control over the sound of your music. You can add all sorts of crazy sounds and even layer up to 64 different instrument tracks on top of each other.

COMPUTER RECORDING SOFTWARE ALLOWS YOU TO RECORD, PRODUCE, AND ARRANGE SONGS IN YOUR BEDROOM.

BANDSPEAK

Musicians often talk about the "arrangement" of a song. This is how and when all of the different beats, sounds, and instruments are used in the song. Computer music recording applications make changing the arrangement of a song quick and easy.

Studio sessions

If home recording doesn't appeal to you, there is another option: the recording studio. Almost all music you listen to, whether it's the pop-folk sounds of Mumford & Sons, the R&B of Beyoncé, or the radio-friendly pop of One Direction, will have been recorded in a studio.

RECORDING IN A STUDIO COULD MAKE YOUR MUSIC SOUND MORE PROFESSIONAL, BUT IT CAN BE EXPENSIVE!

In the studio

Recording studios are rooms or buildings designed with recording and mixing music in mind. They are designed to get the best possible recording of a band or singer. They usually have all the latest recording equipment, from computers and sound cards to the best microphones, keyboards, and electronic gadgets. When you book a recording studio, the price will also include the use of a studio engineer.

BANDSPEAK

A studio engineer is someone who specializes in recording music. The engineer is there to help musicians get the best possible sound from their recordings, sort out technical problems, and assist with the "mixing" of songs.

Quality costs money

Good recording studios are always very busy. This is because they become known for the quality of their recordings. Because of this, famous studios, such as Sunset Sound in Los Angeles and Abbey Road in London, cost enormous sums of money to rent. Big record companies can sometimes spend hundreds of thousands of dollars on studio rental fees when recording an album by a new singer or band.

Not all recording studios are expensive to rent, though. Many major towns and cities boast small studios that offer cheap rates or deals to new bands. There may even be one near you.

IF YOUR BAND IS A SUCCESS, SOON YOU COULD BE RUBBING SHOULDERS WITH TOP BANDS AT STUDIOS LIKE THIS ONE.

You can record your music in many different ways, but which should you choose? If you're still confused, this step-by-step guide should help.

What sort of band or musician are you?

Rapper

Dance producer/DJ

Pop band

Rock band

Singer-songwriter or solo performer

Punk band

Do you have enough money to spend on studio rental fees?

YES

NO

Live recording
Doing a live recording of a performance, either at home or at a concert, will allow you to capture the energy, sound, and style people can expect from your shows. If it doesn't sound right, you can always keep trying until you get a better recording.

Portable multitrack recorder
By using a portable multitrack recorder, you can record as quickly or slowly as you want. If it is good enough for top stars to record their home demos on, it is good enough for you!

What's good?
- They're cheap to buy.
- They're easy to use.
- You can record new songs quickly.
- It can be used to record at home or at a concert.

What's bad?
- It can only record a limited number of instruments, depending on the number of tracks of the recorder.
- It is hard to get a great sound.

What will you need?
To record using this method, you need the following:
- Instruments
- Microphone
- Portable multitrack recorder
- Cables to connect instruments and/or microphone to the recorder.

Should I Choose?

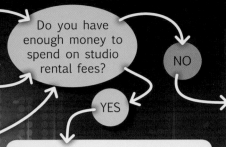

Do you have enough money to spend on studio rental fees?

NO

YES

Recording studio

Recording in a professional studio takes a lot of the hassle out of the process, but it does not come cheap. If there is a studio engineer on hand to help out, great results are much more likely!

What's good?
- They're designed to get the best possible recording of your songs.
- A studio engineer can handle the recording, so you can concentrate on playing.
- Aside from your instruments, the studio should have all the equipment you need.
- Your songs will sound professionally recorded and produced.

What's bad?
- It can be expensive.
- Getting the perfect sound can take time, and more time in studios costs more money.

What will you need?
To use this method of recording you will need:
- To book a studio for the day
- To turn up with your instruments
- To practice and plan beforehand.

Computer recording

By using a computer to record your music, the possibilities for your songs are almost endless. You can try different sounds, use electronic versions of different instruments, and even create great beats without a drummer. It can take time to learn the ropes, but with a bit of practice, it will become second nature.

What's good?
- You can record in your own time and put together great songs piece by piece.
- You have the choice of recording real instruments or using the music-making application's built-in sounds.
- You can quickly rearrange songs by moving sounds around a computer screen.
- You can work alone or with friends.
- You have the ability to create and add amazing sounds, which simply would not be possible with a multitrack recorder.

What's bad?
- Music-making applications can be confusing to use at first.
- Computers can be expensive to buy.
- You can lose the fun of playing together with your friends as a band.

What will you need?
To use this method you will need:
- A computer
- A music-recording application (for example, GarageBand, Logic Pro, Reason, Ableton Live, or Cubase)
- A music keyboard that can be connected to a computer
- A sound card (to plug in instruments or microphones if you want to record them).

RELEASING YOUR MUSIC

Once you have recorded your music, the next stage of the job is to work out how people can listen to it. For musicians, the way they make their music available to other people is known as a release.

The way we were

In the old days, releasing music was an expensive process. You either had to pay the costs of making vinyl records, CDs, or cassette tapes yourself, which was beyond the means of most musicians, or find a record company that would do it on your behalf. These records, CDs, or tapes would then be sold in stores, with any money going back to the record company. Eventually, usually months or years down the line, the musician would get paid.

THE INTERNET MAKES FINDING MUSIC EASY. BUT SOME PEOPLE PREFER TO VISIT A LOCAL MUSIC STORE!

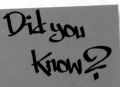

PEOPLE CAN LISTEN TO MUSIC ANYWHERE WITH MP3 PLAYERS.

Release yourself

Things are different now. Since the Internet revolution of the 1990s, fewer people buy music on CD. Instead, most people download MP3s—computer files containing songs that they can play on portable devices. MP3s can cost nothing to make and are easy to release. This is great for musicians wanting to put out music themselves.

Now, you don't need a record label to release your music. If you wanted to, you could record a song in an afternoon and get it up on the Internet within minutes. Releasing songs has never been easier.

Giving it away

The easiest way to release music is to give it away free on the Internet. Every year, millions of people do this, from new bands launching their careers to established bands and even famous pop stars. Today's fast Internet connections make uploading your songs to the web a quick and easy process. Once your MP3s are online, people can listen to them, leave feedback, share them with their friends, and even download them to their phones or computers.

BANDSPEAK

Uploading is the opposite of downloading. It is what people call the process of transferring computer files, such as MP3s and videos, to the Internet.

IZA LACH BECAME KNOWN ACROSS THE WORLD AFTER RAPPER SNOOP DOGG HEARD HER SONGS ONLINE AND SIGNED HER TO HIS RECORD LABEL.

MUSICIAN AND PRODUCER DANGER MOUSE BECAME POPULAR AFTER HE GAVE AWAY SOME OF HIS MUSIC ON THE INTERNET.

Born free

Everyone likes something for nothing, which is why web sites offering free music are so popular. The most popular dedicated music sharing web site is called Soundcloud (www.soundcloud.com). It allows bands to showcase their sounds and find new fans, and it doesn't cost a penny to join.

Where stars are made

Several top musicians have made their name after giving away music on the Internet. Before going on to greater success with his group Gnarls Barkley, electronic musician Danger Mouse became an Internet sensation after giving away an album that mixed together songs from rapper Jay Z (sometimes known as Jay-Z) and rock legends the Beatles. Then, in 2013, Polish singer Iza Lach became a worldwide sensation after rapper Snoop Dogg found her music on Soundcloud. He then signed Lach to his record company. He produced an expensive music video to promote one of her songs.

Sell it yourself

Giving your songs away for free is a great way to get your music out there, and it helps convert listeners into new fans. The next step, though, is to make people pay for the music you have worked so hard to create. That means selling your songs online.

This might seem a bit daunting. There are hundreds of MP3 download stores, but the scene is dominated by a handful of enormous services—the likes of Apple's iTunes, Google Play, and Amazon.

BAND TECH

If you want to get your songs into big download stores, you will need to use a digital aggregator. This is a company that specializes in getting music into many different MP3 stores.

Doing things for free

Getting into the big download stores, which boast billions of songs for sale, is not always the best approach for new bands. Instead, many musicians choose to set up their own online store.

There are many free web sites that help musicians to create their own download store. The most popular is called Bandcamp (www.bandcamp.com). These web sites allow you to choose exactly how much you sell your songs for. They even feature an option called "pay what you want." This allows fans to decide how much they want to pay to download your songs.

Our idea was that everybody paid as much for the music as they felt it was worth. If you think our songs are no good after listening to them, that's a pity indeed. But if you enjoyed listening to the songs, it would be fair to pay something...

Thom Yorke, singer of the band Radiohead

Did you Know?

Radiohead pioneered "pay what you want". In 2007, Radiohead became the first famous band to let fans decide how much to pay to download their new album, *In Rainbows*.

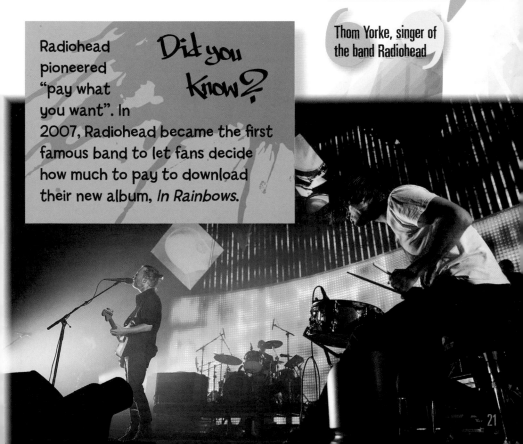

Get physical

Digital music, and MP3s in particular, are incredibly popular. Yet there are plenty of people who prefer to buy, and own, music on what the music industry refers to as physical formats.

Promotional tool

There are many benefits to putting your songs onto CD or record. For starters, it will give you something to sell to friends, family, fans, and people who attend your live shows.

CDs and records can also be used as a promotional tool. Many new bands manufacture (or "press up," in music industry speak) CDs and give them away to influential people, such as DJs, radio personalities, bloggers, and concert promoters. If you give people a CD, it is more likely that they will listen to it than if you send them MP3 download links.

A LOCAL DJ CAN GET YOUR SONG HEARD ALL OVER YOUR AREA.

Cheap and cheerful

Making CDs is not as expensive as you think. Getting 100 professional-looking CDs manufactured costs roughly $400. Records are much more expensive, but they can be sold at a higher price and appeal to underground music fans and collectors. Making 100 records can cost anything upward of $900. A cheaper option is cassette tapes. This is a format that was very popular in the 1980s and has recently enjoyed a comeback. Making tapes is a good way to appeal to collectors who are looking for something different.

CDS ARE USUALLY MADE AT SPECIALIZED "PRESSING PLANTS," LIKE THIS ONE IN FRANCE OWNED BY THE COMPANY MPO.

BANDSPEAK

Physical formats get this name because you can touch them, unlike MP3s, which are simply an electronic version of a song stored on a computer or phone. Popular physical formats include compact discs (CDs) and vinyl records (pressed black plastic discs popular with DJs).

Thinking big

If you have some success selling your own CDs or records, the next step is to get them sold in stores. So, how would you go about getting your music to the masses?

Some small, independent record stores take CDs from individual bands or artists, but most don't.

Read the label

This is where record companies, sometimes called record labels, come in. They specialize in recording music, producing CDs, and then getting them into stores. They also work hard to promote their releases so that they sell more. At a basic level, record companies make money by recording music by bands and selling it on to stores, which then sell it to the public.

Majors and minors

The world's biggest record companies—so-called major record labels—put out thousands of releases every year. Yet for every major record company, there are hundreds of smaller labels that put out new releases only five or six times a year.

Many bands start their own record label to put out their music. It's not that difficult, and it gives them control over what they release and when. If things go well, they often start putting out music by other bands they like or by friends from the music scene. This way of releasing music is very popular in underground music communities, such as the indie rock and dance scenes.

Smaller record labels do not deal directly with record stores and online stores. Instead, they use another company, called a distributor, to do it for them. Like digital aggregators, distributors specialize in selling music to stores.

How music distribution works

Musician
Records songs and provides them to the record label.

Record label
Takes the musician's songs and turns them into releases. The music is then sent to two different places.

Distributor
Takes CDs and records from the record label and then tries to sell them into stores.

Digital aggregator
Takes MP3 copies of the same music and gets them to download stores.

Online stores
Online stores such as Amazon sell huge numbers of CDs every year.

Download stores
Stores like iTunes and Google Play sell millions of MP3 downloads every year.

Chain music stores
In addition to big chain stores, which have branches in many different towns and cities, distributors also sell to supermarkets.

Streaming services
Digital aggregators also provide music to streaming services (where the music is "streamed" over the Internet) such as Spotify.

Local record stores
Small, independent record stores are few and far between today, but they still play an important role by selling less well-known music to fans.

PROMOTING YOUR MUSIC

You have recorded some music, put it on the Internet, and sold a few CDs to friends, family, and fans. So, what next?

If you are successful, your songs might have been downloaded a few hundred times, and you will have gotten rid of all of those CDs. If you are not successful, you will find yourself scratching your head and wondering what went wrong. The thing is, you have done nothing wrong. Nearly all musicians get frustrated that their music is selling slowly. It is easy to think that people aren't interested in what you are doing.

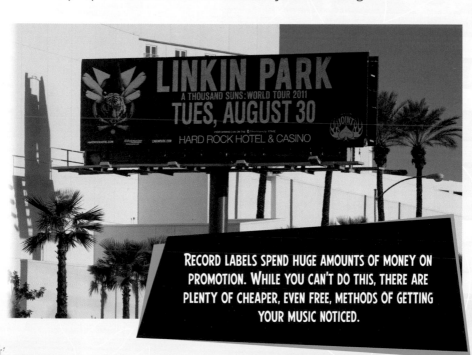

RECORD LABELS SPEND HUGE AMOUNTS OF MONEY ON PROMOTION. WHILE YOU CAN'T DO THIS, THERE ARE PLENTY OF CHEAPER, EVEN FREE, METHODS OF GETTING YOUR MUSIC NOTICED.

Hard questions

Ask yourself this question: Do people know about your music? If they don't know who you are, what sort of music you make, and where to find it, there is no way they will find it, download it, and become a fan of your band. The music industry is a very competitive business, and everyone wants to get their music heard. If you are going to sell more music, play bigger concert venues, and build a fan base, you need to work hard at promoting your band. And working hard means working *really* hard.

BIG STARS SPEND MILLIONS OF DOLLARS PROMOTING THEIR MUSIC, OFTEN THROUGH LARGE-SCALE TOURS AND HIGH-PROFILE LIVE APPEARANCES. BUT YOU DON'T HAVE TO DO THIS...

Did you know?

Promotion can cost a lot of money. According to a recent music industry report, major record labels spend between $100,000 and $530,000 on promoting each new band they sign.

Think big!

Thankfully, you don't need to spend hundreds of thousands of dollars to raise awareness of your band. There are plenty of things that you can do for free that will give your band a greater chance of standing out from the crowd.

Big on the web

The Internet has completely changed the world of music. People used to discover music through radio stations, newspapers, or music magazines. Most people now find new music on the Internet.

THANKS TO SMARTPHONES AND DIGITAL CAMERAS, VIDEOS OF BANDS PERFORMING LIVE CAN BE RECORDED AND UPLOADED TO THE INTERNET ALMOST INSTANTLY.

Get online!

If you want people to find your music, then you need to think about how and where they can find it online. Music sharing sites such as Soundcloud are a good start, but if you really want to make an impression, you will need more than this. You could start by creating a web site or blog for your band, which would be a permanent home on the Internet for your music. Your web site could contain a short history of the band, lists of other bands you like, music clips, photos, and links to other places people can find your music online, such as your Soundcloud page.

According to research in 2012, over half of all teenagers in the United States listen to music by looking at songs on the video sharing web site YouTube.

TODAY, MOST MUSIC PROMOTION TAKES PLACE ON THE INTERNET. TEENAGERS DISCOVER LOTS OF THEIR MUSIC THROUGH SOCIAL NETWORKS AND VIDEO SHARING SITES.

Get on the networks

Once you have your own blog or web site, the next step is to create profile pages for your band on social networks. Facebook reportedly has over 1 billion users worldwide and has become one of the greatest ways of promoting music. Facebook users can "like" band pages to receive updates about their music, concerts, videos, and releases.

Another great tool for promoting music is the video sharing web site YouTube. You could make and upload videos of your band performing new songs, practicing at home, or even being interviewed.

INSPIRED

THE ARCTIC MONKEYS

The Arctic Monkeys are one of the best-known young rock bands in the world. Had it not been for the Internet, though, they would probably still be playing concerts in tiny venues in their hometown of Sheffield, England.

Small beginnings

In 2004, the Arctic Monkeys were barely known outside Sheffield, where they had built up a small following of fans who attended their performances. Their luck began to change when they started giving away CDs of their songs at concerts. Some local fans made MP3s of these songs and put them on the Internet. The same fans then created a profile page for the band on the social network MySpace.

New Fans

Although they didn't know it, the Arctic Monkeys' fan base was growing. Soon, more people appeared at their concerts—people who knew the words to their songs. These new fans had found out about the band on MySpace. By early 2005, they had become an Internet sensation and were asked to play on the unsigned band stages at big music festivals.

The Arctic Monkeys performed at the opening ceremony of the 2012 London Olympics, in front of an estimated worldwide television audience of 900 million people.

Did you know?

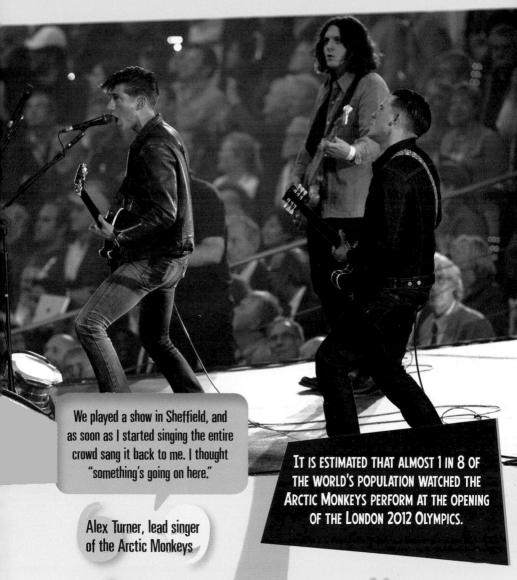

We played a show in Sheffield, and as soon as I started singing the entire crowd sang it back to me. I thought "something's going on here."

Alex Turner, lead singer of the Arctic Monkeys

IT IS ESTIMATED THAT ALMOST 1 IN 8 OF THE WORLD'S POPULATION WATCHED THE ARCTIC MONKEYS PERFORM AT THE OPENING OF THE LONDON 2012 OLYMPICS.

Record breakers

It just got better from there for the Arctic Monkeys. The first two songs they released after signing with Domino Records, "I Bet You Look Good on the Dancefloor" and "When the Sun Goes Down," both were successful. Thanks to the Internet, they had become superstars almost overnight.

Marketing your band

So, you have recorded some music, put it on the Internet, set up your own band web site, and created profiles on social networks. The next step is to think about marketing your band.

LIKE MANY STARS, SINGER KE$HA TRAVELS AROUND THE WORLD PROMOTING HER MUSIC IN TV, RADIO, AND OTHER MEDIA INTERVIEWS.

Megabucks marketing

Major record companies spend millions every year on marketing their bands. They spend money on placing advertisements on the Internet and on television, putting up posters, and sending music writers on trips around the world to interview top bands.

You don't have to spend this sort of money to get great results. There are lots of things you can do for free to raise awareness of your music.

Spread the word

One of the first things you should do is send your music to people who can give it some coverage. First, that means contacting people who write about music for newspapers, magazines, blogs, and web sites. You should also try sending your music to radio stations and local DJs. Many local radio stations have shows dedicated to new music, while DJs can play your songs at events.

There are many other things you can do to market your music, from making your own music videos and arranging appearances in local record stores to asking concert promoters for slots at local music festivals. If you spend some time thinking about it, you will soon realize there are lots of cool and interesting things you can do to promote your band.

MANY YOUNG BANDS APPEAR AT LOCAL MUSIC FESTIVALS TO GAIN SOME PUBLICITY.

BANDSPEAK

"Marketing" is the name given by businesses to the activities that are involved in making people aware of a product. In music terms, this means any activities you do in order to try to sell downloads, CDs, or concert tickets.

Building a Fan Base

The most famous bands, singers, and musicians in the world have thousands, sometimes millions, of fans scattered around the globe. These are people who support their favorite bands by buying downloads, CDs, T-shirts, and concert tickets. Fans spread the word about bands' concerts, releases, and videos by telling their friends, either in person or on the Internet. If your band is going to be successful, you need fans. That means working hard to build up a fan base.

TAYLOR SWIFT IS KNOWN FOR SPENDING TIME MEETING HER FANS.

LADY GAGA HAS A SPECIAL RELATIONSHIP WITH HER FANS. SHE CALLS THEM HER LITTLE MONSTERS.

Finding Fans

Turning people who listen to your music into fans can be tricky. You want listeners to become active fans, because they will become more supportive of your band. Instead of occasionally buying one or two of your songs, fans will buy all of them. They will turn up to your concerts and festival performances. They will also try to persuade their friends to become fans, who in turn might persuade their friends. All bands need fans, which is why they are so valued by musicians. With so many bands competing for fans, what can you do to stand out from the crowd?

BANDSPEAK

A fan is anyone who is particularly enthusiastic about something, be it a band or sports team. Collectively, all a band or sports team's fans are called a fan base. A fan base could be a handful of people who regularly attend a band's concerts or thousands of people around the world who keep track of their favorite singer's music over the Internet.

Get connected

Once upon a time, top bands very rarely got to connect with their fans. These days, all that has changed. Now, using social media, fans and musicians can talk on the Internet.

BandSpeak

Social media refers to Internet services, such as Twitter and Facebook, that promote interaction between people. Typically, social media services allow people to post short updates (such as "posts" on Facebook) on which other users can comment.

Stay safe online

Many children and teenagers have gotten into trouble after meeting up with people they have spoken to online. Try to avoid agreeing to meet up with strangers you have talked to online. If you have agreed to meet up, take an adult with you.

THE INTERNET IS A GREAT WAY TO CONNECT WITH FANS. BUT STAY SAFE ONLINE: ALWAYS INVOLVE AN ADULT IF YOU ARE THINKING OF MEETING SOMEONE.

Get closer to fans

Many top musicians use social media to connect directly with their fans. Since fans can sign up to "follow" their favorites on Twitter and Facebook, it gives musicians a chance to say what they are up to, when they are performing live, and when their songs are released. They can also answer questions posed by fans. Twitter is very popular with both musicians and music fans. In fact, musicians are so popular on Twitter that the company has even launched an application to help users find great new music.

Get tweeting!

Your band might struggle to attract millions of followers on Twitter, but it will allow you to build a strong relationship with your fans. There are also lots of other social media services you can use to update fans on what you are up to. You could share photos of shows and recording sessions on Instagram (www.instagram.com), share your favorite things on Pinterest (www.pinterest.com), or build a profile on ReverbNation (www.reverbnation.com).

RAPPER SEAN "DIDDY" COMBS IS ONE OF THE MOST POPULAR MUSICIANS ON TWITTER. AT THE END OF 2013, HE HAD NEARLY 10 MILLION FOLLOWERS.

INSPIRED

AMANDA PALMER

If you want an example of how using social media can change a musician's fortunes, take a look at the career of American singer Amanda Palmer. Palmer was originally a singer with the band The Dresden Dolls. She has become one of the most popular underground musicians thanks to the way she connects with fans on the Internet.

AMANDA PALMER STARTED OUT AS ONE HALF OF THE DRESDEN DOLLS. SHE LATER FOUND GREATER FAME AS A SOLO PERFORMER.

Big tweeter

Palmer is a huge fan of social media, particularly Twitter. She now has close to a million followers on Twitter, an amazing number for somebody whose music is not that well known. The reason she has so many followers is the way she uses the service. So far, she has used it to perform live, using video services such as UStream, sell T-shirts directly to fans, and organize "online hangouts" with fans, where she answers questions and plays songs.

The most positive [thing about using Kickstarter] was feeling directly connected to my fans without having to deal with...a [record] label who only cared about sales and money.

Amanda Palmer

Money maker

The story gets even more impressive. On her web site, she claims she once made $20,000 in one day simply using social media. She started off by offering fans the chance to buy a T-shirt featuring a design suggested by one fan. She then offered to answer questions, sing songs, and sign postcards for any fan who sent her $20. She then decided to organize and sell tickets for a special, fan-only concert.

PALMER REGULARLY PERFORMS SMALL SHOWS FOR FANS. SHE ARRANGES THESE THROUGH SOCIAL MEDIA.

Rewarding your fans

Amanda Palmer understands that creating a close bond with fans is important. The closer your fans feel to you, the more likely it is that they will continue to support you. Because of this, it is never a bad idea to thank them for supporting you.

Get creative

There are many different things you could do to reward your fans for their loyalty. You could offer them free MP3 downloads of brand new tracks, put on concerts just for Twitter followers, or offer them the chance to meet the band. You could start your own fan club or allow dedicated fans special access to unseen video clips.

Did you know?

To celebrate the release of her seventh album, *Unapologetic*, in 2012, Rihanna held a special competition for fans. The lucky winners joined the star singer on a trip to see her perform in seven different cities around the world in seven days.

RIHANNA OFFERS FANS THE CHANCE TO MEET HER IF THEY WIN COMPETITIONS RUN BY HER RECORD LABEL.

Believe in your band!

You may never make enough money to be able to fly fans around the world with your band, but you have to think big. If you follow the advice in this book, work hard, record good songs, and promote your music, there is no reason why your band can't be an enormous success. In a few years, you might be rewarding your fans by putting on an extra-special concert somewhere magical. Now wouldn't that be something to celebrate?

BIG BANDS SUCH AS THE ROLLING STONES HAVE PLAYED SMALL SHOWS FOR FANS.

The three most popular Twitter profiles in the world belong to musicians. Katy Perry, Justin Bieber, and Lady Gaga each have over 35 million Twitter followers.

Did you Know?

QUIZ

Putting together a marketing plan for your band can be time consuming and confusing for beginners. Try this multiple-choice quiz to help decide which route you should take.

1 How much spare time do you have?
   a) Lots.
   b) A fair amount.
   c) Enough, though I mostly spend that spare time with friends.

2 How creative are you?
   a) I think I'm very creative.
   b) I think I'm fairly creative.
   c) I don't think I'm creative.

3 How good are you with computer technology (computers, smartphones, tablets)?
   a) I'm very good with computers.
   b) I'm comfortable using computers.
   c) I'm not that confident with computers.

4 Are you a good writer?
   a) I'm very good with words.
   b) I really like writing and think I'm okay with words.
   c) I sometimes struggle with writing.

5 Are you confident talking to people that you don't know?
   a) I'm better at talking with people on the Internet.
   b) I prefer writing, but I'm willing to talk to people to get things done.
   c) I'm happy talking to people.

6 Do you like to go out and meet other people in the local music scene?
   a) I don't mind, but I'd rather be practicing with the band or checking out new music online.
   b) I enjoy meeting new people and talking about music.
   c) I love making new friends in the music scene and talk to people from other bands all the time.

7

Do you read a lot of music blogs, web sites, and magazines?

a) I don't read many magazines, but I'm always looking at blogs and web sites.

b) When I'm not playing music, I spend a lot of time reading about music.

c) I'd rather experience music, either by playing it myself or hearing other people play it.

8

If you had to describe the sound of your band in three words, how easy would you find it?

a) I could do that.

b) I'd find it very easy.

c) I could do it, but I'd rather have 10 words.

Answers

IF YOU ANSWERED MOSTLY AS:

You are a born social media whizz! You are comfortable with computers, write fairly well, love finding new music online, and know what is hot and what is not. You should focus your marketing efforts on building a good web site for your band and interacting with fans on social media.

IF YOU ANSWERED MOSTLY BS:

You are a closet music writer! You love reading about music, are passionate about writing, and don't mind talking to people in the music industry. These are great qualities for somebody who promotes music to writers, radio stations, and DJs. You should concentrate on writing short articles about your band and sending them, along with your music, to magazines, newspapers, blogs, and web sites.

IF YOU ANSWERED MOSTLY CS: You are a go-getter! Instead of sitting at a computer writing or building web sites, you like to be out and about, meeting new people and hanging out at concerts with music scene friends. These are great qualities in the music industry, where it takes confidence and a bit of hustle to get things done. You should use these qualities to talk enthusiastically about your band to venue owners, concert promoters, and local record store owners. Sometimes success in the music industry boils down to "who you know," rather than "what you know." Get talking and see if you can secure some slots at local music events.

GLOSSARY

album collection of songs, usually released on CD, record, or MP3 download

beats rhythmic or drum-like sounds

cassette tape format for storing and playing back recorded music, popular in the 1970s, 1980s, and 1990s

demo demonstration recording, usually the first recording of a song done by a band. It is also used to refer to any recording that has not been professionally produced.

digital aggregator company that specializes in getting MP3 music files into download stores

distributor company that specializes in selling CDs and records to record stores, which then sell them to the public

DJ short for "disc jockey." Someone who plays recorded music to people for a living.

download process of transferring something stored on the Internet onto a home computer, smartphone, or tablet computer

download store web site that specializes in selling MP3 music files

major record label large company, usually with offices around the world, that specializes in releasing and selling recorded music. Major labels dominate the music industry.

marketing activities involved in making people aware of a product and ensuring it is available to buy

mixing way of turning a multitrack recording into a finished song

MP3 type of computer document for storing and playing recorded music

multitrack process of recording music onto many different tracks, in order to have more control over the sound of the finished song

music festival large event, usually held over several days, featuring performances from lots of bands, musicians, and DJs

portable something that can easily be carried around

promotion anything done to raise awareness of something— for example, a band, CD, or concert

prospective something or someone that may become something— for example, people watching a band perform live for the first time are prospective fans

record pressed black disc, made out of a type of plastic called vinyl, on which recorded music can be stored and replayed. Records are popular with DJs.

record label company that specializes in releasing and selling music

record store store that sells music, usually CDs and records

recording process of capturing a performance of a song, so that it can be put onto CD or record, or turned into an MP3 file, which people can then listen to on their own devices

recording studio room or building specially designed for recording music

social media Internet services, such as Twitter and Facebook, that specialize in allowing people to communicate quickly with each other

social network web site, such as Facebook, that allows people in different places to connect with each other using messages, online chat, and so on

studio engineer somebody who specializes in the recording of music and whose job it is to make songs sound great

synthesizer electronic instrument, based around a piano keyboard, that allows musicians to play and record lots of different sounds

underground music music that goes against what most people are listening to

upload process of transferring something stored on a home computer, tablet, or smartphone onto the Internet

vocal musician's term for singing or rapping, for example— the sound of the voice

FIND OUT MORE

Books

Anniss, Matt. *Start a Band!* (Find Your Talent). Mankato, Minn.: Arcturus, 2012.

Anniss, Matt. *Start a Blog!* (Find Your Talent). Mankato, Minn.: Arcturus, 2012.

Web sites

diymusician.cdbaby.com
This blog, which is updated regularly, features lots of great advice for musicians who want to promote and market their music themselves.

www.gmarts.org
Find hints and tips for teenagers starting bands at this web site, which also includes great information about writing and recording music.

www.hypebot.com/hypebot/2010/03/6-rules-to-make-a-band-website-that-rocks.html
If you are looking to create a web site for your band, this article has some excellent advice.

www.stanford.edu/~kenro/beginnerdigitalaudio.html
This is a step-by-step introduction to recording music onto a computer.

DVDs

Band Slam! (2010, rated PG)
Vanessa Hudgens from *High School Musical* stars in this story about a teenage band that forms in school.

That Thing You Do! (1997, rated PG)
Watch this story of a fictional 1960s pop rock band and how it found success.

Further research

There are lots of great web sites out there for aspiring musicians. This includes Internet message forums, where more experienced bands and musicians will gladly offer you advice.

Many community organizations offer short classes for teenagers and young people on how to record music and the basics of music production (the process of creating great recorded songs). These classes are usually run by colleges, community centers, or small, local recording studios. There might be something happening in your area, so ask other local musicians to see if they have heard anything.

If you are interested in making a career out of music production or promotion, you can find lots of information on the Internet. Start with the books and DVDs listed here.

If you enjoy writing about music, there are many music blogs and web sites you might be able to write something for. If this interests you, e-mail the people behind your favorite blogs and web sites and ask if they are looking for writers.

Index

Abbey Road 13
Amazon 20, 25
apps 10, 15
Arctic Monkeys 30–31
arrangements 11

Bandcamp 21
Beyoncé 12
Bieber, Justin 41
Biffy Clyro 6
blogs 28

careers in music 47
cassette tapes 16, 23
CDs 16, 17, 22, 23, 24, 25,
    26, 30, 33
cell phones 6, 10, 18
chain stores 25
Chuck D 20
Combs, Sean "Diddy" 37
community classes 47
computer recording 7,
    10–11, 12, 15

Daft Punk 10
dance music 7, 10, 24
Danger Mouse 19
demos 8
digital aggregators 20, 24,
    25
distributors 24, 25
DJs 33
download stores 17, 20,
    21, 25
Dresden Dolls 38

Facebook 29, 36, 37
fan base 27, 30, 34–41
free music 18, 19, 20

Google Play 20, 25

indie rock 24
Instagram 37
Internet 17, 18–21, 28–29,
    30, 31, 32

iPads 10
iTunes 17, 20, 25

Kane, Dom 7
Ke$ha 32
keyboards 7, 10, 12, 15
Kickstarter 39

Lach, Iza 18, 19
Lady Gaga 35, 41
launching new careers 4,
    5, 27
Libertines, The 8
live recordings 14
London 2012 Olympics
    30, 31

master records 9
mixing 7, 12
MP3 stores 20, 25
MP3s 6, 7, 17, 18, 20, 22,
    23, 30, 40
multitrack recorders 8–9,
    14
Mumford & Sons 12
Muse 8
music festivals 30, 33, 35
music sharing web sites
    19, 28
MySpace 30

One Direction 12
online safety 36
online stores 24, 25

Palmer, Amanda 38–39, 40
"pay what you want" 21
Perry, Katy 41
physical formats 22–23
Pinterest 37
playback 9
portable recorders 8, 14
profile pages 29, 30
promotion and marketing
    22, 24, 26–29, 32–33

radio stations, local 33
Radiohead 21
record labels 4, 5, 13, 16,
    24, 25, 26, 27, 32, 39
record stores 16, 24, 25,
    33
recording studios 8, 10,
    12–13, 15
releasing music 16–19, 24,
    25
ReverbNation 37
Rihanna 40

selling your music 20, 21,
    24–25
Snoop Dogg 18, 19
social media 29, 30, 36–39,
    41
sound cards 11, 12, 15
Soundcloud 19, 28
streaming services 25
Strokes, The 8
studio engineers 12, 15
Sunset Sound 13
Swift, Taylor 34

tablets 10, 18
Twitter 36, 37, 38, 39, 40,
    41

uploading music 18
UStream 38

videos 19, 27, 28, 29, 33,
    38
vinyl records 16, 22, 23, 25
volume 9

web sites, creating 28

Yorke, Thom 21
YouTube 27, 28, 29